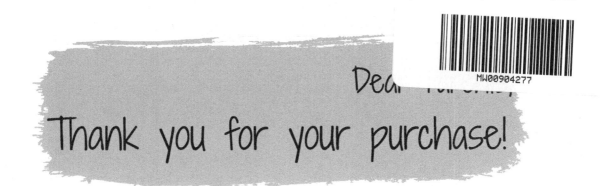

Dear Parents,

Thank you for your purchase!

We would love to see your child's creations!

Tag us in your picture by using the following hashtag on social media:

 #GoPoPublish

Or simply text us an e-mail at:

 GoPoPublish@gmail.com

this book belongs to

. . . .

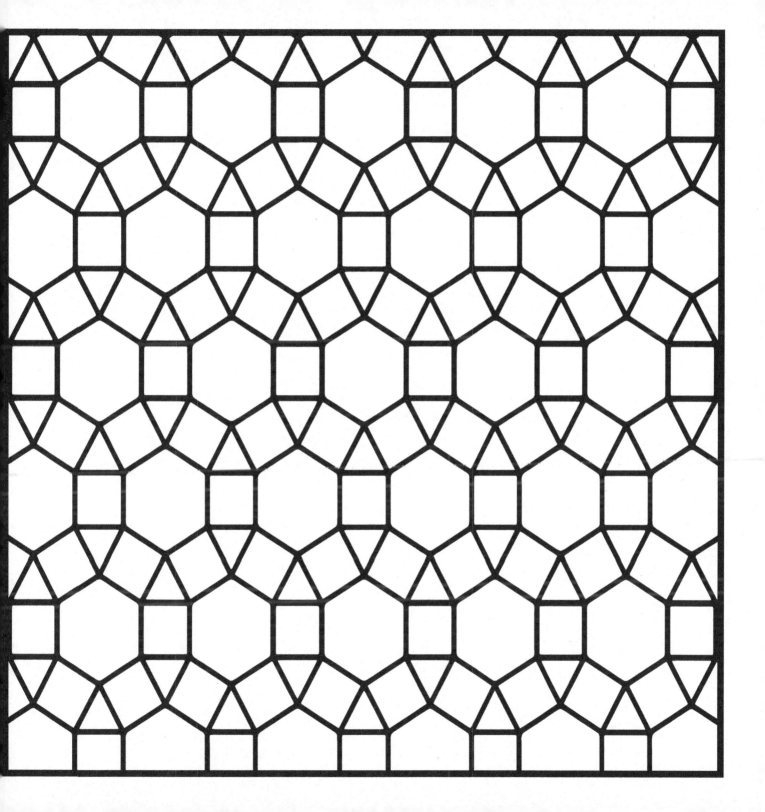

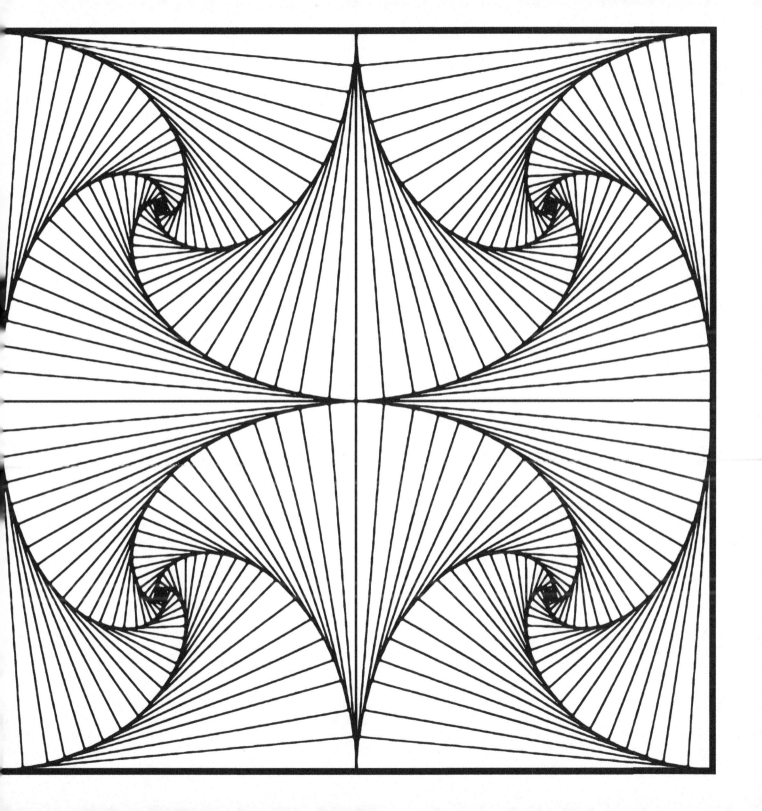

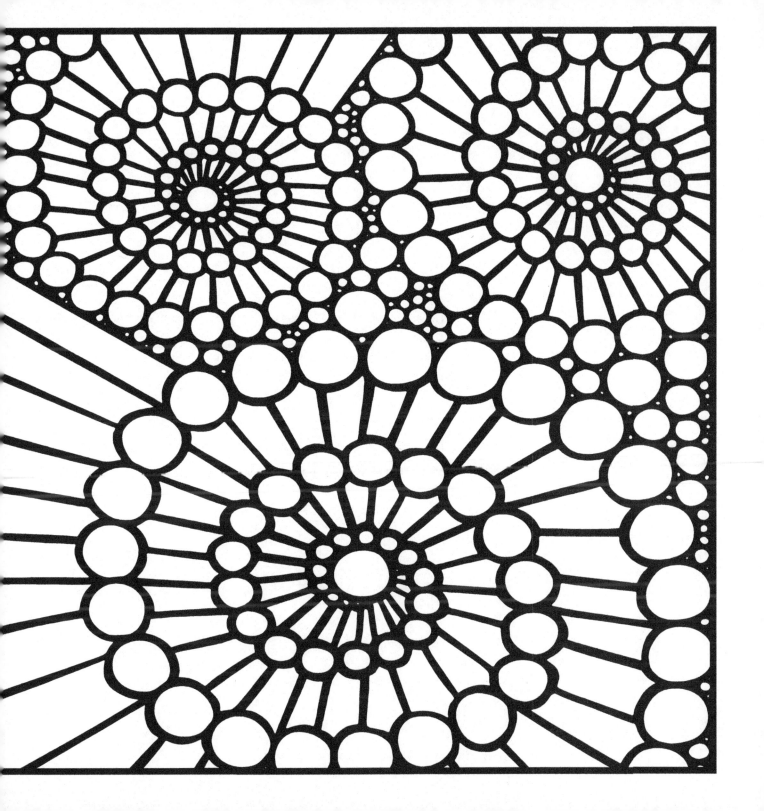

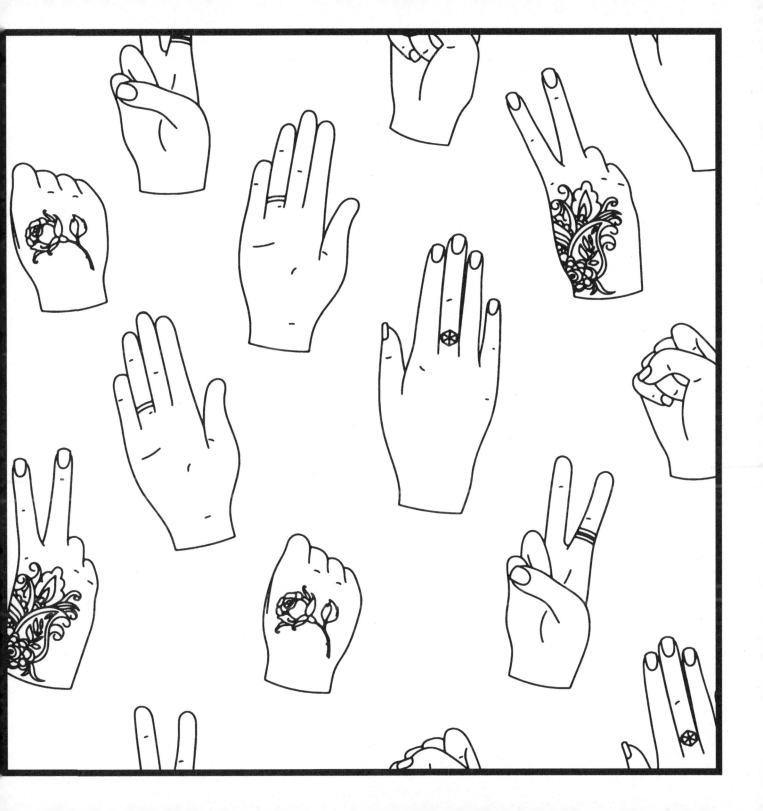

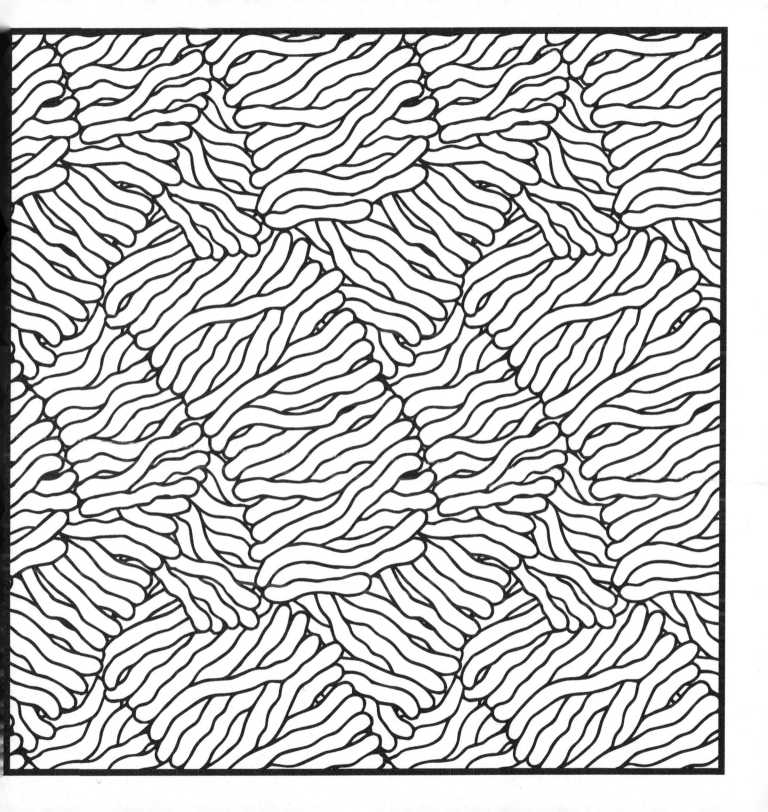

This Diploma Is Proudly Presented To:

DIPLOMA

Has Completed This Beautiful Coloring Book With Joy And Fun

Presented on: _____

_____

Parent's Signature

Made in the USA
Coppell, TX
10 November 2024

39938630R00059